Mastering Volume Profile in Day Trading

Spotting Hidden Support and Resistance, Understanding Market Structure with Value Area and Volume Nodes for High-Probability Trade Opportunities

by

Nathaniel J. Brooks

DISCLAIMER

This book is only designed for educational and informational purposes. It is intended to illustrate trading ideas, systems, and market insights gained through study and practice. It is not designed to provide personalised financial guidance or suggestions.

This book does not provide any financial, investing, legal, or trading advice. All techniques, charts, examples, and scenarios are offered solely for educational illustration and should not be regarded as recommendations to buy, sell, or hold any financial asset.

Trading in the foreign exchange market and other financial instruments entails risk, including the loss of funds. No method, strategy, or example presented in this book can guarantee success. Market conditions vary, and previous performance is no guarantee of future results or illustrations.

Readers are solely responsible for their trading decisions, risk management, and outcomes. Trading should only be done with funds that you can afford to lose. Readers are encouraged to seek financial expert guidance as needed.

All chart drawings in this book are based on publicly available market price data and are intended solely as analytical examples for educational purposes. Charts, tools, platforms, brokers, and software are only mentioned for instructional purposes. The author is not

Table of Contents

INTRODUCTION

The first time I lost $800 in fifteen minutes, I realized something was fundamentally wrong with my approach to FX trading. There I was, sitting at my screen, with what I believed was the ideal configuration - a gorgeous support level that had held three times before. The technical analysis appeared faultless. Every indicator screamed "BUY. However, the market ripped through my support as if it did not exist.

That awful morning in 2016 altered everything for me. You've undoubtedly been there as well, watching your meticulously drawn support and resistance lines crumble while you try to understand why. Most traders blame themselves. They believe they need better indicators, more intricate techniques, or that they are simply not cut out for trading.

I realized the actual issue was not my discipline or approach. It was my understanding of what drives markets.

Traditional chart analysis reveals where price has gone, but it does not explain why some levels hold while others collapse quickly. You build horizontal lines based on past highs and lows, thinking that they would serve as barriers in the future. They do not always work. Often, they do not. This inconsistency frustrates traders because there is no way to foresee which levels will be important.

The volume profile shifted my entire perspective on market behavior. Instead of guessing where support and resistance could form, I learned to identify them where they already exist: hidden in plain sight within the volume data.

Most traders don't understand that price swings aren't random. Every pip that goes up or down is due to buying and selling activities. When enormous sums of trading take place at specific price levels, those levels act as magnets for future price movement. The market has memory, which is stored in volume.

After three years of struggle with traditional analysis, I discovered volume profile practically by mistake. A mentor mentioned it during a webinar, so I spent the weekend researching how it worked. The concept appeared too simple to be effective. How could looking at volume clusters help my trading results?

My first week employing the volume profile resulted in more consistent profits than the prior month combined. Not because I suddenly improved my trading skills, but because I finally grasped what the market was saying me.

The volume profile displays the hidden architecture of price movements. When you consider where institutional money has accumulated positions, where retail traders are frequently stranded, and where smart money defends its levels, trading becomes less about prediction and more about probability.

You'll learn how to identify support and resistance levels that do not display on normal price charts. Because most traders cannot detect these hidden levels, they frequently present the most dependable trading chances. You will know exactly where the genuine fighting zones exist while everyone else draws the same obvious lines.

Simply understanding the Value Area concept changed my perspective on market structure. This zone, where 70% of a session's volume trades, serves as a gravitational center for price action. When prices move away from this area, they tend to be brought back. When it breaks out strongly, it frequently results in tremendous progress in that direction.

Point of Control levels - the particular price at which the maximum volume is transacted - become critical battlegrounds. I've seen price respect these levels with near mathematical accuracy, bouncing off them several times before breaking through with conviction.

But here's something that took me years to completely understand: volume profile isn't just another indication to add to your charts. It's an entirely different method of interpreting market behavior. You are not looking for entry signals in the traditional sense. You're finding the fundamental underpinnings that support or oppose price fluctuations.

This book will show you how to see markets via volume-focused lenses. You'll understand why some levels persist while others fail immediately. More importantly, you will learn to identify high-probability setups before the majority of traders do.

The trip is not always smooth. There were months when I questioned whether the volume profile was genuinely superior to traditional ways. However, some trades went against me. The difference was that my winners grew in size and frequency, but my losses shrank and became more predictable.

By the end of this book, you'll have a methodical method for reading market structure that goes much beyond surface-level price movement. You'll learn how to identify hidden support and resistance, how to employ Value

Areas for exact entrances and exits, and how to recognize volume signatures that presage large price swings.

Your trading experiences will never be the same.

CHAPTER ONE

Volume Profile Revolution in Forex Trading

Most forex traders approach the market backwards. Based on patterns, signs, or gut emotions, they analyze price movements and try to predict where they will go next. This strategy continuously fails because it ignores the underlying driver that drives all price movements: volume.

You've undoubtedly spent many hours sketching support and resistance lines on your charts. Perhaps you have studied candlestick patterns, moving averages, or Fibonacci retracements. These tools are functional, but they are missing the most important piece of information: where the real money is transferred.

Why Traditional Support and Resistance Fails for Most Traders

Traditional horizontal support and resistance levels are based on a simple concept: if a price has previously bounced from a level, it may do so again. This sounds reasonable, yet it is fundamentally faulty. You are making decisions based on where the price touched, rather than where actual trading activity occurred.

I discovered this the hard way during my second year of trading. Over the course of two weeks, the EUR/USD had rebounded three times from 1.1200. Every technical analysis book stated that this was solid support. When the price approached that level again, I increased my long positions. The level shattered like tissue paper, and my account suffered a substantial loss.

The issue was not my analysis, but my understanding of what causes support and resistance. Price levels that appear important on charts frequently have little actual trading volume behind them. Meanwhile, levels with high volume concentrations are invisible to conventional technical analysis.

Figure 1: The EUR/USD daily chart shows that typical horizontal resistance has been breached, causing severe upward movement.

Volume Profile Difference

By showing you where the majority of trading actually occurred, volume profile changes everything. Instead of guessing which price levels are important, you can observe exactly where institutional money, retail traders, and market makers have concentrated their efforts.

When I initially came across volume profile analysis, I was doubtful. How could something so easy provide an advantage that millions of traders were missing? The solution comes in understanding that most retail traders do not have access to high-quality volume data, and even fewer understand how to analyze it appropriately.

The volume profile exposes three essential characteristics that price charts cannot show. First, it determines where the most trading activity occurred over specified time periods. Second, it displays the price levels at which buyers and sellers were most active. Third, it provides the Point of Control, which is the exact price at which the biggest volume of trades occurred.

Figure 2: GBP/USD daily chart with volume profile overlay, showing high volume node and value area

Volume Reveals What Price Action Cannot Show

Price action tells you what happened, but volume explains why it happened with such certainty. When you notice a strong price movement accompanied by high volume, you know institutional money was driving it. When price changes on low volume, they are most typically driven by retail mood and are susceptible to reversal.

The actual breakthrough occurs when you realize that volume determines future support and resistance. Areas where extensive trading occurred become reference points for future price action. Traders remember these levels. Algorithms are programmed to respond to them. The market creates memories around high-volume price zones.

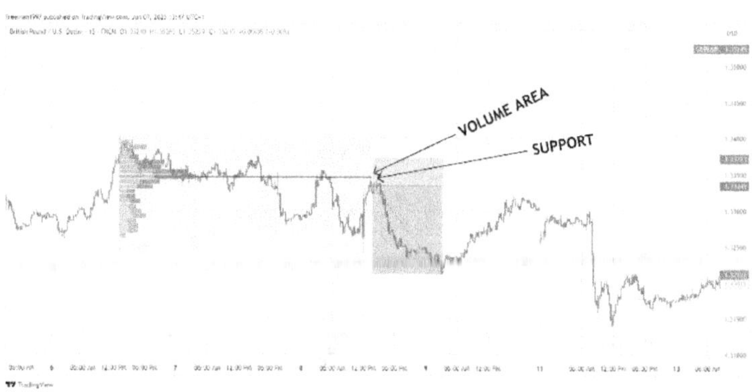

Figure 3: GBP/USD m15 chart shows how past high-volume locations (seen in volume profile) later operate as support

Time-Based Versus Volume-Based Analysis

Traditional charting is time-based. Each candle represents a certain time period: one minute, one hour, and one day. This technique considers all time periods equally, regardless of how much trading occurred during those times.

Volume-based analysis is activity-driven. Instead of when something happened, it focuses on where trading activity was concentrated. A tranquil Asian session hour with low volume has the same visual impact as a tumultuous London session hour with high trading activity. This skews your understanding of market behavior.

When you switch to volume-based thinking, you can perceive the market's underlying structure. You discover the price zones where real money changed hands, where institutions established positions, and where retail traders are frequently caught.

Setting realistic expectations.

Volume profile is not a quick fix that will make you profitable overnight. It's a complicated analytical tool that takes time and effort to perfect. You'll need to change your perspective on how markets work and what makes price levels meaningful.

The learning curve differs for each trader. Some people get the concepts immediately, while others need months to completely incorporate volume analysis into their trading strategy. Your training in traditional technical analysis may actually slow down the process because you'll need to unlearn some ingrained behaviors.

You should expect a gradual improvement in your ability to detect high-probability scenarios. Your win rate may not rise drastically, but your risk-to-reward ratios should improve greatly. You'll quit getting stuck at obvious levels and instead place yourself where the genuine edge resides.

Figure 4: GBP/USD 1-hour chart with both standard support/resistance lines and volume profile data, demonstrating the disparities between where retail traders normally set their levels and where volume clusters.

What You'll Achieve After Mastering This Approach

Understanding its core concepts is the first step toward mastering volume profile. Once you understand how volume influences market structure, you'll never look at price charts the same way. You'll get the ability to foresee where institutional money will defend or attack price levels, providing you a huge advantage over traders who only use traditional approaches.

Your trading style will become more systematic and less emotive. Instead of praying that obvious support and resistance levels persist, you'll know exactly where the market has shown true interest based on trading volume. This knowledge converts speculation into a determined likelihood evaluation.

CHAPTER TWO

Understanding Volume Profile Fundamentals

The volume profile significantly alters how you interpret market activity by presenting trading data in an entirely different style. Instead of showing volume as bars beneath price action, it rotates the data 90 degrees and presents it horizontally across price levels.

You are looking at a histogram that extends from the price axis. The longer the horizontal bar at any given price level, the higher the volume traded at that price. This simple rotation exposes patterns that are otherwise unseen on traditional charts.

What Does Volume Profile Actually Measure in Forex Markets?

Volume in forex trading represents the actual quantity of currency moved at each price level over the time period you choose. A thick horizontal bar stretching from a specific price indicates that hundreds or millions of dollars changed hands at that same level.

The currency market differs from the stock market in terms of volume data. You are not seeing the total global volume for a currency pair, as this is impossible to track across all banks and financial institutions worldwide. Instead, you can see volume from your broker's liquidity providers and associated networks.

This constraint does not reduce the efficacy of volume profile analysis. The volume data you receive still represents considerable trading activity and appropriately depicts where key participants concentrated their trades. Large institutions, hedge funds, and algorithmic trading systems leave distinct traces in this data.

The Structure of a Volume Profile Chart

Each volume profile chart has distinct components that work together to indicate market structure. The profile itself is depicted as a series of horizontal bars extending from the price axis. These bars form a bell curve or skewed distribution pattern that reveals where trading activity clustered.

You'll observe that some price levels have extremely short bars, indicating low trading activity. Other levels show thick, prominent bars indicating high volume concentration. The overall shape of the profile conveys a story about market behavior over the time period you specify.

The width of your volume profile varies depending on the time period you choose. A daily profile illustrates where volume is concentrated on a single trading day. A weekly profile shows the volume distribution for an entire week. Each time frame yields unique insights into market structure and player behavior.

High Volume vs. Low Volume Nodes Explained

High Volume Nodes (HVNs) are price levels where heavy trading activity occurred. These look as thick horizontal bars in your volume profile. HVNs often serve as support and resistance since they identify regions where numerous traders have a vested interest.

When the price approaches a High-Volume Node, it usually pauses, bounces, or consolidates. Market participants who have previously traded at these levels will defend or increase their positions. This produces natural support and resistance zones, which traditional chart analysis frequently overlooks.

The volume profile shows Low Volume Nodes (LVNs) as thin horizontal bars or gaps. Price moves fast through these zones because few traders have positions to defend. LVNs frequently become zones of significant price movement rather than consolidation areas.

Understanding the distinction between the two node kinds is critical for trade planning. You should enter positions around HVNs where you expect support or resistance, and avoid placing stops in LVNs where prices may gap through fast.

Point of Control: The Market's Favorite Price Level

The Point of Control (POC) is the one price level that represents the volume of trades throughout the time period you choose. This level appears as the longest horizontal bar on your volume profile and frequently serves as a significant reference point for future price action.

I've noticed that prices consistently move approaching POC levels. When prices move away from the POC, they are frequently drawn back like a magnet. When price breaks firmly through a POC level, it typically indicates a dramatic shift in market sentiment.

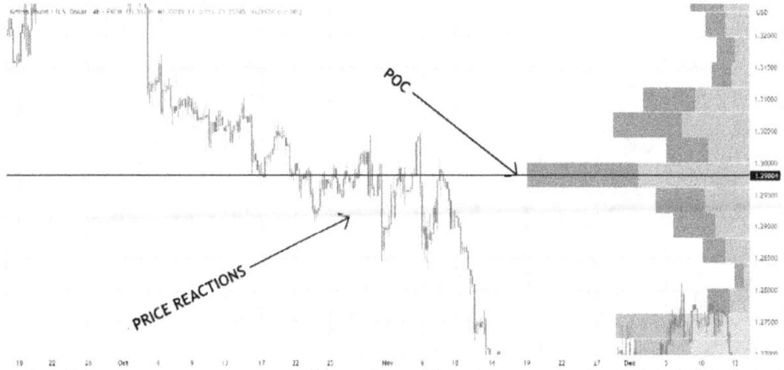

Figure 5: GBP/USD 4-hour chart with POC clearly marked and showing many price interactions with this level

[Chart Reference (Fig 5): The chart shows price bouncing off or being attracted to the POC level].

POC levels from past time periods are still relevant for extended periods. A daily POC may influence price action for several days. A weekly POC can be meaningful for weeks. These levels become part of the market's memory and continue to elicit price movement long after they were established.

Value Area Concept and the 70% Rule

The Value Area includes the price range in which 70% of the total volume transacted over the time period you specify. This zone usually encircles the POC and represents the area where the majority of market participants agreed on fair value.

Value Area High (VAH) and Value Area Low (VAL) are marked as the limits of Value Areas. These levels frequently serve as support and resistance, but their significance goes beyond mere bounce points. They show the consensus range in which the majority of trading activity occurred.

When prices trade within the Value Area, market conditions are usually balanced. When prices move outside of this range, it indicates that new information or institutional activity is pushing the market to a new value consensus.

Reading Volume Distribution Patterns

Volume profile patterns show varying market circumstances and participant behaviors. A balanced profile has a conventional bell curve distribution, with most volume grouped around a core price level. This demonstrates efficient price discovery and balanced trading circumstances.

Skewed profile results show that buyers or sellers prevailed over the time period. An upward skew indicates that buying pressure drove prices higher as volume grew. A downward tilt suggests that selling pressure is focused at the lower levels.

Dual-distribution profiles show two different volume clusters separated by lower volume zones. These patterns frequently emerge during transitional market periods, when two distinct value sectors vie for dominance.

Understanding these patterns allows you to evaluate market sentiment and forecast future price moves based on the volume distribution.

CHAPTER THREE

Set Up Your Volume Profile Trading Platform

Your trading platform influences the quality of volume data you'll receive and how well you can use volume profile analysis. Not all platforms provide correct volume information, and many brokers supply restricted or synthetic data that will not provide you the advantage you require.

The setup process entails more than simply putting indicators. You must understand which data sources provide accurate information, how to configure your charts for optimal analysis, and which settings are critical for profitable trading.

Selecting the Appropriate Broker and Platform for Volume Data

Volume quality varies greatly among brokers. Some offer tick-by-tick data from key liquidity sources, while others forecast volume based on price fluctuations. This distinction influences every part of your volume profile analysis.

ECN brokers often provide better volume data because they combine data from several liquidity sources. Market maker brokers frequently show artificial volume that does not reflect genuine trading activity. When comparing volume profiles between platforms, you'll see a clear difference.

I switched brokers three times before discovering one that regularly gave correct volume data. The change in trading outcomes was significant after I had access to solid information. Your volume profile analysis is only as good as the data that drives it.

Look for brokers who provide Level II data or market depth information. These characteristics suggest access to institutional-grade volume feeds. Avoid brokers who offer only basic retail platforms with insufficient data transparency.

Setup Instructions for MT4, MT5, and TradingView

MetaTrader 4 requires third-party volume profile indicators because the platform does not natively support this functionality. Download trusted indicators from experienced developers who offer frequent updates and customer support. Free indicators frequently lack the precision necessary for professional trading.

MetaTrader 5 has basic volume profile tools, although they are limited when compared to specialized platforms. The built-in Market Profile indicator provides basic functionality, but comprehensive analysis requires extra tools.

TradingView provides the most complete volume profile tools for retail traders. The Volume Profile indicator offers extensive customization possibilities and precise data visualization. Their Fixed Range Volume Profile tool enables you to evaluate certain time periods with precision.

Configure TradingView's volume profile with three critical settings: increase the number of rows to at least 100 for extensive analysis, enable the Point of Control line, and activate Value Area highlighting. These modifications give the granular data required to make informed trading decisions.

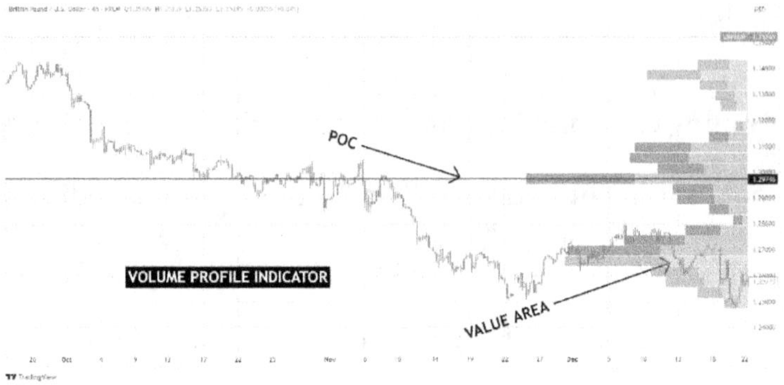

Figure 6: GBP/USD 4-hour chart on TradingView show properly configured Volume Profile indicator with POC line and Value Area highlighted

Setting Up Volume Profile Indicators Correctly

Most traders use default settings without understanding how they impact analysis accuracy. The number of rows in your volume profile impacts how many price levels it evaluates. There are too few rows that do not have important volume clusters. Too many rows provide noise, obscuring meaningful patterns.

For most time periods, start with 100-150 rows. Daily charts may need fewer rows, however intraday charts frequently demand more detail. Adjust based on the price range you're looking at and the volatility of your preferred currency pairs.

Value Area proportion requires careful consideration. The normal 70% setting is adequate for most markets, however some traders prefer 68% or 75%, depending on their approach. Test different percentages to see what works best for your trading strategy.

Time Period Settings That Do Matter

Fixed Range Volume Profile evaluates time periods that you specify. This tool is quite useful for analyzing how volume behaved during important market events or trading sessions. You can isolate New York session activity, London session volume, or any custom time period.

Session Volume Profile generates new profiles for every trading session. This method enables you to understand how volume patterns change throughout the day and identify which sessions offer the best trading chances for your strategy.

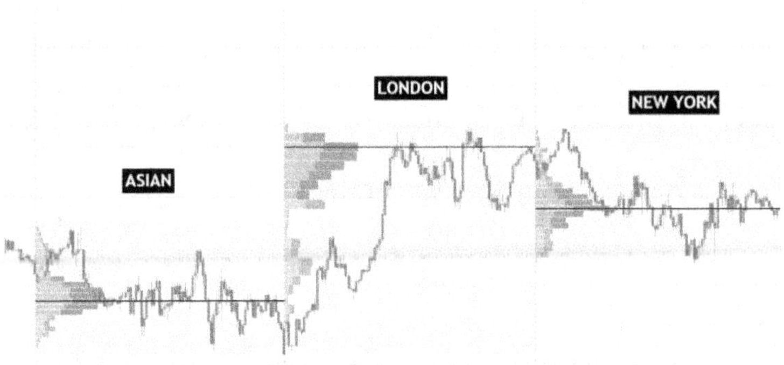

Figure 7: GBP/USD chart showing Session Volume Profile, with unique profiles for Asian, London, and New York sessions

[Chart Reference 3 (Fig 7): The chart should show separate volume profiles for each significant trading session, with obvious changes in volume distribution.]

The Visible Range Volume Profile adapts in real time based on what is currently showing on your screen. This dynamic technique is effective for active trading, but it can be confusing when scrolling over past data. When real-time volume analysis is required, use this setting.

My Platform Setup After Over 10 Years of Refinement

I use TradingView as my primary charting platform, with an MT5 backup for order execution. Multiple timeframes are active simultaneously: daily charts for overall market structure, 4-hour charts for swing analysis, and 1-hour charts for exact entries.

Every timeline shows a distinct volume profile setting. Daily charts show long-term volume distribution using Visible Range profiles. Four-hour charts show Fixed

Range profiles for the previous week's activities. Session profiles are shown on 1-hour charts to help track intraday patterns.

Color coding allows for faster interpretation. High volume sections are highlighted in vivid colors that stick out quickly. Value Areas employ semi-transparent fillers that do not conceal price action. POC lines appear in contrasting colors that are apparent on all chart backgrounds.

Common Setup Mistakes That Cost Traders Money.

Using volume profiles on timescales shorter than 15 minutes frequently results in incorrect data. The volume samples grow too small to exhibit meaningful patterns, and noise drowns out true signals. Maintain greater timeframes until you have mastered the fundamentals.

Overlapping too many volume indicators causes chart clutter, which impedes decision-making. Three volume profiles are allowed each chart, which gives enough information without overwhelming your analysis. More indicators do not necessarily imply greater analysis.

Ignoring broker-specific volume constraints causes false confidence in your analysis. Understand the volume data your broker provides and its limits. Some brokers aggregate volume differently, which affects your profile's accuracy.

Wrong time zone settings cause distortions in session-based volume profiles. Ensure that your platform displays times in your broker's time zone, or convert manually. Misaligned sessions can cause London volume to appear during Asian hours, dramatically altering your analysis.

Regular platform maintenance ensures that your volume analysis is correct. Indicators should be updated as new versions become available. To avoid display issues, frequently clear stored data. Back up your specific configurations to avoid losing optimized settings when the platform upgrades.

CHAPTER FOUR

The Psychology of Volume Nodes

Volume nodes emerge due to human psychology and institutional behavior patterns that are consistent across all financial markets. Understanding why traders cluster their activity at specific price levels provides insight into potential market movements in these zones.

Every volume node resembles a battlefield where buyers and sellers are fiercely competing. The thicker the node, the more intense the struggle. These psychological fingerprints are not lost when the price goes away; they remain in the market's memory.

Why Do Certain Price Levels Draw Massive Volume?

Round numbers naturally attract trading activity because human psychology prefers prices that are easier to remember. At levels such as 1.2000, 1.1500, or 110.00 in forex pairings, you may see increases in volume. These psychological levels become self-fulfilling prophecies when traders around the world place orders at the same evident points.

Previous big highs and lows produce a lot of volume since these levels represent crucial decision points. When price reaches a previous high, bulls who missed the initial move have another opportunity to buy. Bears who bought at the top can now exit their losing positions. The convergence of several incentives results in volume clustering.

Higher-timeframe support and resistance zones concentrate volume since institutional traders use these levels to develop their positions. A daily support level may show little action on 15-minute charts, but tremendous volume accumulation when studied over several hours or days.

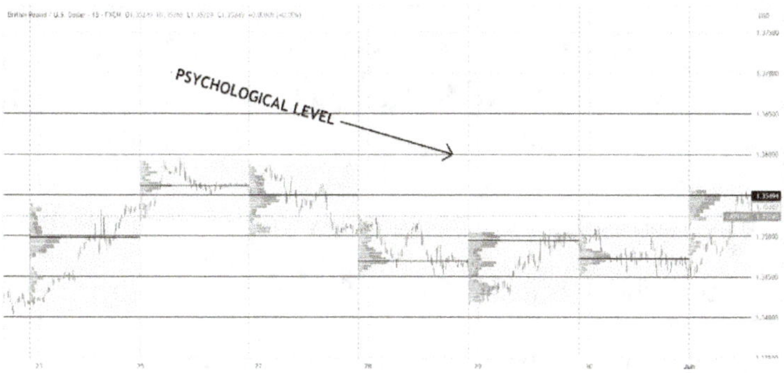

Figure 8: GBP/USD chart with volume clustering around round numbers and past important highs/lows.

[Chart Reference (Fig 8): The chart shows clear volume spikes at psychological levels like 1.34500 and 1.3500, indicating how these levels attract excessive trading activity.

Economic announcement levels generate temporary volume magnets. When important news breaks, prices frequently respond wildly before settling into a new range. The levels at which this settling happens frequently become future volume nodes because they represent the market's new consensus on fair value.

Institutional Behavior and Volume Clustering.

Large institutions cannot execute trades at single price points without causing the market to move against them. They instead progressively develop positions across price ranges, creating the volume clusters we observe in our profiles.

When a hedge fund needs to buy $500 million in EUR/USD, it cannot simply place a big order on the market. They break this position down into smaller chunks and execute over hours or days, creating consistent volume at multiple price levels within a range.

Central bank interventions leave distinct volume characteristics that are relevant over time. When the Swiss National Bank abandoned the EUR/CHF peg in 2015, the large volume generated set reference levels that dominated price behavior for months.

Algorithmic trading systems contribute to volume clustering by carrying out similar methods at predetermined levels. When numerous algorithms trigger at the same time, they cause dramatic volume spikes that serve as new reference points for future trading.

The Story of Smart Money Versus Retail Money

Smart money acts differently than retail traders, resulting in predictable volume patterns. Retail traders often chase momentum in the other way, but institutional players tend to buy weakness and sell power.

When volume clusters toward the bottom of price ranges, it typically implies institutional accumulation. Smart money leverages retail selling pressure to develop positions at advantageous prices. The volume node formed throughout this process serves as a foundation for future price support.

Retail money focuses on breakout points and momentum extremes. Retail traders rush in when prices break through evident levels of resistance, creating volume spikes at precisely the wrong time. These volume clusters frequently represent reversal points rather than continuation zones.

Distribution patterns reveal smart money quitting positions and retail money entering. Heavy volume at price highs, paired with subsequent weakness, indicates institutional selling into retail purchasing pressure. These nodes usually serve as resistance during subsequent rallies.

The Day I Caught a 200-Pip Move With Structure Analysis

The EUR/GBP scenario emerged during a period when most traders experienced regular consolidation. Price had been trading in a range for two weeks, and traditional analysis showed that the sideways movement would continue. However, my volume analysis told a different story.

Daily volume profiles demonstrated POC movement toward the upper end of the range. Each day's Point of Control was somewhat higher than the day before, despite the price remaining within the established limits. This migration pattern revealed institutional accumulation that was not obvious using typical chart analysis.

The Value Area patterns supported the accumulation idea. While prices solidified, Value Areas gradually increased and began to overlap less with earlier times. The combination of POC migration and Value Area progression foreshadowed coming structural disruption.

When price finally broke above the range resistance, I felt confident in my long position because volume analysis suggested underlying institutional activity. The break resulted in a sustained 200-pip move as concealed accumulation drove price discovery to new value areas.

Checklist for Building a Market Structure

Effective market structure analysis necessitates a thorough assessment of different volume elements. Begin by identifying the present Value Area location in relation to recent price movement. This determines whether price is trading inside established value areas or venturing into new value territory.

Examine POC positioning throughout several timeframes to better identify institutional reference points. Daily POCs provide short-term structural direction, whilst weekly POCs offer a longer-term perspective. Alignment of periods helps structural analysis.

Examine volume distribution patterns for indications of accumulation, distribution, or equilibrium. Each pattern predicts varied future price behavior and aids in the development of effective trading techniques. Document these patterns to get practice with pattern recognition.

Monitor Value Area acceptance and rejection patterns to determine market attitude about new price levels. Sustained acceptance confirms structural changes, whereas frequent rejection suggests the persistence of the existing structure.

Keep track of volume vacant areas and gaps that could represent breakout zones. These areas frequently give the path of least resistance when the market structure changes. Identifying them ahead of time provides you a strategic advantage when a break occurs.

CHAPTER FIVE

Identifying Hidden Support and Resistance

Hidden support and resistance levels exist in plain sight, buried inside volume data that most traders never look at. Because these levels are invisible to traditional technical analysis methods, they frequently provide the most consistent trading opportunities.

You're up against millions of other traders that use the same clear horizontal lines at prior highs and lows. The actual advantage comes from identifying levels that aren't marked on everyone else's charts but have a remarkable consistency in influencing price behavior.

Going Beyond Obvious Horizontal Lines.

Traditional support and resistance identification is based on where prices have previously struck particular levels. This technique ignores a critical aspect of trading activity. A price level that was briefly struck with low volume has significantly less significance than a level where tremendous trading occurred over time.

Volume-based support and resistance levels frequently exist at prices that have never shown clear rejections on regular charts. Price could have spent a lot of time consolidating in a range, resulting in significant volume accumulation on the side without decisive bounces. These zones act as potent magnets for future price activity.

Gap areas on traditional charts can occasionally hold the strongest hidden support and resistance levels. While prices never traded in these gaps, volume analysis illustrates the theoretical levels at which significant trading interest existed. When the price falls into these zones, the reaction can be significant and immediate.

Multi-timeframe volume analysis exposes levels that are invisible on single timeframe charts. A 15-minute volume cluster may appear tiny until you learn it corresponds exactly to weekly volume concentration. This confluence produces hidden levels with incredible storage capacity.

How Volume reveals Invisible Price Barriers.

Volume accumulation patterns show where institutional money concentrated its trading activities. These patterns generate invisible limits that prices follow long after the initial accumulation period has ended. The market has a collective memory of these important trading zones.

When you see persistent volume at certain price levels without any clear price reactions, you've discovered possible hidden support or resistance. These levels show areas where significant players steadily increased or diminished their positions, laying structural underpinnings for future price behavior.

The distribution volume patterns illustrate where smart money departed positions during periods of seeming strength. During this dispersion, the price may have remained higher, disguising the underlying selling pressure. When prices return to these distribution zones, hidden resistance frequently emerges unexpectedly.

Absorption patterns show when one side of the market took all available volume from the other. These zones cause imbalances, which price must finally address. Hidden support forms exist in which buying absorbs all selling pressure, even if the price does not instantly bounce.

The Impact of Old Value Areas as Future Battlegrounds

Long after they were founded, previous Value Areas retain their significance. These zones represented market participants' fair value consensus, and this collective memory does not fade as prices move away. When prices return to old Value Areas, they frequently elicit powerful reactions.

Value Area edges from high timeframes produce very effective hidden levels. A weekly Value Area High may provide resistance on intraday charts for several weeks after it has occurred. Most day traders will miss this level since they are focused on shorter timeframes, providing you an important advantage.

Overlapping Value Areas from various time periods result in zones of outstanding significance. When a daily Value Area coincides with a weekly Value Area, the combined influence creates levels capable of stopping or reversing large price moves. These confluences are invisible to traders who use traditional tactics.

Gap Value Areas develop when prices shift so quickly that they bypass traditional value zones. These overlooked value areas frequently act as magnets, drawing price back to allow correct value discovery. The hidden support or resistance that emerges in these zones can be quite strong.

Volume-Based Support That Does Not Appear on Naked Charts

Naked charts show only price fluctuations, without the underlying volume background that drives them. Volume-based support levels frequently occur at prices with few evident reactions, making them invisible to traditional analysis but extremely powerful in practice.

Algorithmic volume clusters form hidden levels in which computer-driven trading systems focus their activity. These levels do not always correspond to clear price reactions, but they do show zones where systematic buying or selling occurred. When prices revisit these areas, algorithmic systems frequently reawaken.

Institutional anchor points emerge as large players gain considerable positions over time. These levels may not show spectacular price reactions during the accumulation phase, but they serve as reference points for institutions to defend or target in future trading. The hidden resistance or support that emerges can persist for months.

News-driven volume accumulation produces levels that traditional analysis entirely ignores. When important economic news cause momentary volatility, volume concentration during price discovery creates hidden levels that influence future price behavior.

My Method for Marking the Levels That Actually Hold

For identifying and marking hidden support and resistance levels, I employ a three-tier technique. Tier One levels are derived from current period volume analysis, which show immediate volume clusters and Value Area limits. These provide short-term reference points for day trading decisions.

Tier Two levels are derived from higher timeframe volume analysis, usually one or two timeframes above my trading charts. To identify these levels, a 4-hour trader would look at daily and weekly volume profiles. Tier Two levels frequently provide the most dependable hidden support and resistance.

Identifying confluence zones where various timeframes show volume concentration, Tier Three levels integrate multi-timeframe analysis with historical volume data. These levels have tremendous holding power and frequently represent important turning points in market structure.

Color-coding distinguishes across level kinds and timeframes. To ensure rapid awareness, current temporal levels employ strong colors. Higher timeframe levels use muted colors that do not clutter the chart but are still easily visible. Colors are used to illustrate the significance of historical confluence zones.

Real Examples of Major Currency Pairs

At prior monthly Value Area highs that lasted for extended durations, EUR/USD frequently exhibits hidden resistance. These levels frequently halt rallies that break past evident daily resistance, trapping traders who focus solely on shorter timeframes. Barriers that can persist for quarters are created by the monthly volume memory.

The GBP/USD pair shows strong hidden support at weekly Point of Control levels from significant moving periods. These POC levels frequently provide the basis for further accumulation when the pair enters consolidation stages. These levels' hidden nature makes them very beneficial for establishing positions.

USD/JPY demonstrates how intervention volume produces long-term hidden levels. Central bank involvement during currency interventions creates volume signatures that influence price behavior for years. These intervention levels are hidden from most traders, yet they continue to influence large price moves long after the original intervention occurred.

CHAPTER SIX

Market Structure from A Volume Perspective

When studied through volume analysis rather than typical price action approaches, market structure is seen in a different way. Volume distribution patterns reveal the fundamental causes driving price movements and assist in identifying structural changes before they become apparent on standard charts.

Understanding how volume influences market structure provides you with early notice of trend changes, consolidation periods, and breakout opportunities. You'll view the market's intentions through the prism of actual trading activity, not just price swings.

Volume Distribution-Based Trend Identification

Strong trending markets have distinct volume distribution patterns that differ significantly from consolidating markets. During healthy uptrends, volume focuses at higher price levels as institutional money accumulates positions in each new value area.

Volume-based trend analysis looks at where trading activity clusters rather than the price direction. The trend lacks institutional support and is susceptible to reversal, as evidenced by price achieving greater highs while volume concentration remains at lower levels.

Trending volume profiles often have skewed distributions, with volume concentrating in the trending direction. Within each profile period, an uptrend should have increased volume at higher price levels. When this pattern breaks, the trend structure weakens, even if the price continues to move in the same direction.

Distribution volume patterns indicate trend fatigue before price action confirms it. When you see high volume concentration at trend extremes, followed by price decline, institutional money is most likely abandoning positions. This sets the stage for trend reversals.

Volume gaps between trending legs show market structure details that price charts overlook. These gaps indicate areas where price moved too quickly for normal value creation, creating zones that frequently draw future price movement for proper value discovery.

How Value Areas Shift Across Market Phases

Value Areas travel in predictable patterns under various market conditions. Trending markets have Value Areas that shift continuously in the direction of the trend, with little overlap between consecutive periods. This evolution implies a good trend development with appropriate institutional engagement.

Consolidating markets have overlapping Value Areas that cluster around the same price levels over multiple time frames. This overlap suggests that buyers and sellers agree on fair value within a specific range. The width of these overlapping areas reflects the degree of the consolidation.

Transitional periods between trending and consolidating phases exhibit various value area patterns. The overlap steadily reduces or rises, offering early indicators of shifting market circumstances. These transitions frequently provide the best trading chances for experienced traders.

Value Area acceptance occurs when prices establish new areas and maintain them over time. This acceptance confirms structural shifts and new trend directions. Rejection occurs when prices briefly enter new value areas before fast returning to prior zones.

Volume Profile Signatures for Accumulation and Distribution

Accumulation phases reveal particular volume profile traits that smart money develops while establishing positions. Volume concentrates in the lower price ranges as institutional buyers absorb selling pressure from retail traders. The generated profiles exhibit significant volume clustering below current market values.

Distribution patterns emerge when savvy money quits positions during periods of apparent market strength. Volume concentrates at higher price levels while price rises, creating a misalignment between volume location and price direction. These patterns frequently presage big reversals.

Balanced volume profiles suggest effective price discovery using normal bell curve distributions. These patterns indicate fair value agreement between buyers and sellers, which frequently results in range-bound trading circumstances until external factors upset the balance.

Composite volume analysis examines different time periods to uncover long-term accumulation and distribution patterns. Weekly composite profiles may reveal accumulation that is unseen on daily charts, providing insight into institutional positioning over time.

Identifying Market Structure Breakdowns Before They Happen

Volume profile analysis gives early warning signals for market structure breaks by recognizing specific patterns. Even if price has not yet verified the break, structural changes are likely to occur when volume concentration diverges significantly from known patterns.

POC migratory patterns indicate shifting market dynamics before evident breaks emerge. When Point of Control levels repeatedly shift in the same direction over numerous time periods, the market is laying new fundamental groundwork. This movement frequently precedes significant trend changes.

Value Area expansion or contraction shows changes in volatility, which frequently precede structural fractures. Expanding Value Areas indicate increased uncertainty and the possibility of major movements. Contracting areas suggest consolidation, which usually leads to eventual breakouts.

Volume void identification identifies areas where structural fractures are likely to occur. These gaps represent price levels with little historical trading activity, creating zones where prices can move quickly without encountering major resistance or support.

The Day I Caught a 200-Pip Move with Structure Analysis

The EUR/GBP scenario emerged during a period when most traders experienced regular consolidation. Price had been trading in a range for two weeks, and traditional analysis showed that the sideways movement would continue. However, my volume analysis told a different story.

Daily volume profiles demonstrated POC movement toward the upper end of the range. Each day's Point of Control was somewhat higher than the day before, despite the price remaining within the established limits. This migration pattern revealed institutional accumulation that was not obvious using typical chart analysis.

The Value Area patterns supported the accumulation idea. While prices solidified, Value Areas gradually increased and began to overlap less with earlier times. The combination of POC migration and Value Area progression foreshadowed coming structural disruption.

When price finally broke above the range resistance, I felt confident in my long position because volume analysis suggested underlying institutional activity. The break resulted in a sustained 200-pip move as concealed accumulation drove price discovery to new value areas.

Checklist for Building a Market Structure

Effective market structure analysis necessitates a thorough assessment of different volume elements. Begin by identifying the present Value Area location in relation to recent price movement. This determines whether price is trading inside established value areas or venturing into new value territory.

Examine POC positioning throughout several timeframes to better identify institutional reference points. Daily POCs provide short-term structural direction, whilst weekly POCs offer a longer-term perspective. Alignment of periods helps structural analysis.

Examine volume distribution patterns for indications of accumulation, distribution, or equilibrium. Each pattern predicts varied future price behavior and aids in the development of effective trading techniques. Document these patterns to get practice with pattern recognition.

Monitor Value Area acceptance and rejection patterns to determine market attitude about new price levels. Sustained acceptance confirms structural changes, whereas frequent rejection suggests the persistence of the existing structure.

Keep track of volume vacant areas and gaps that could represent breakout zones. These areas frequently give the path of least resistance when the market structure changes. Identifying them ahead of time provides you a strategic advantage when a break occurs.

CHAPTER SEVEN

High-Probability Setup Identification

High-probability setups occur when various volume-based components align to create circumstances with favorable risk-to-reward attributes. These setups do not guarantee profits, but they do provide mathematical advantages that accrue over time if used regularly.

Instead than depending on gut impressions or insufficient analysis, you should use methodical criteria to evaluate probable trades. Profitable traders frequently distinguish themselves from failing traders by identifying and executing only the highest-probability chances.

The Anatomy of a Perfect Volume Profile Settings

Perfect volume profile setups combine structural features to form many layers of confluence. Price must be approaching a large volume-based level, with higher timeframe analysis indicating a definite directional bias. The setup requires both technical structure and volume confirmation to work in tandem.

Market context has a significant impact on setup quality. The same volume pattern may have a high probability in trending situations but become unreliable after consolidation. Understanding the current market phase allows you to alter expectations and position sizing accordingly.

Volume momentum gives extra validation for high-probability setups. When volume rises as the price approaches crucial levels, it indicates institutional engagement, which can generate big movements. Decreasing volume frequently suggests a lack of conviction and reduced probability results.

Multi-timeframe alignment considerably improves setup probability. When daily, 4-hour, and 1-hour volume profiles all support the same directional bias, the combined influence results in significant setups with increased profit potential.

My 5 Criteria System for Filtering Trades

The first criterion demands a clear volume-based level designation within your analysis timeline. This level must be substantial enough to influence price behavior, and it is usually a point of sale, Value Area boundary, or major volume node. Weak volume levels do not provide a significant advantage for profitable trading.

The second requirement necessitates a greater period context that supports your planned trading orientation. If you're contemplating a long trade, higher timeframes should show bullish structure or, at the very least, no strong negative signs. Fighting in a greater timeframe structure diminishes probability greatly.

The third criterion requires volume momentum confirmation at the setup level. Volume should rise as the price approaches your goal level, showing institutional interest. Decreasing volume indicates a lack of participation and affects setup reliability.

The fourth criterion demands explicit risk management parameters and rational stop placement. Your stop should be placed beyond the volume-based level, with adequate buffer to prevent premature triggering. If reasonable stop placement results in unfavorable risk-reward ratios, avoid the transaction.

The fifth criterion assesses confluence with other technical factors. Price action cues, momentum indicators, or fundamental catalysts that correspond to your volume analysis increase the probability of a setup. Single-factor setups rarely provide a significant advantage for consistent profitability.

POC Bounces vs. POC Breaks: Understanding the Difference

POC bounces occur when the price approaches the Point of Control levels and then reverses without considerably penetrating. These bounces occur as institutional traders defend their reference levels, resulting in natural support or resistance. Volume often rises during successful bounces as defense mechanisms activate.

POC breaks require consistent volume and institutional participation to be successful. When price breaks through POC levels with conviction, it typically indicates structural changes in market sentiment. These breaks frequently result in rapid progression to the following big volume level.

Volume features distinguish between expected bounces and potential breaks. Bounces show volume surges at the POC level, followed by an instantaneous reverse. Breaks show consistent volume as the price pushes through and beyond the POC level with little hesitation.

Time spent at POC levels provides further insights about expected outcomes. Quick touches frequently result in bounces, as the level maintains its defensive features. Extended consolidation at POC levels indicates growing pressure, which typically results in eventual breaks.

Value Area Edges: Precise Entry Points

Value Area High (VAH) and Value Area Low (VAL) provide specific entry locations for high-probability setups. These borders indicate the limits where 70% of trading volume occurs, making them suitable inflection points for price behavior. Institutional algorithms frequently place orders on these mathematically significant levels.

Rejection at Value Area margins provides exceptional risk-reward opportunities. When the price approaches VAH and shows rejection indications, short positions can be entered with stops close above the level. Similarly, VAL rejections provide extended opportunities with tight stop placement beneath the boundary.

Acceptance beyond the Value Area's edges indicates the possibility of expanded movements. When price closes above VAH or VAL levels with volume confirmation, it frequently moves to the next important volume cluster. These acceptance moves provide trending trade chances.

False breaks at Value Area edges result in some of the greatest probability mean reversion trades. When price momentarily breaches VAH or VAL but immediately returns to the Value Area, it frequently results in powerful moves back toward the Point of Control.

Volume Node Confluences that Rarely Fail

Multiple volume nodes aligning at the same price levels result in confluence zones with exceptional holding power. When daily POC coincides with a weekly high volume node, the combined institutional interest makes it extremely difficult to breach these levels without major fundamental drivers.

Cross-timeframe Value Area confluences provide some of the most dependable trading chances. When the 4-hour Value Area Low coincides with the daily POC, the mathematical probability of the level remaining stable increases significantly. These confluences frequently signal significant turning points in short-term price activity.

Historical volume confluences occur when current price levels approach those where considerable volume concentration occurred in past weeks or months. The market's memory of these levels creates magnetic effects that pull price movement even after a long time has passed.

Multiple forms of volume analysis are combined at single price levels in institutional confluence zones. When POC, Value Area edges, and High Volume nodes cluster around the same price, institutional algorithms and human traders use these levels to make decisions.

Why Most Traders Are Stopped Out and How to Avoid It

Most traders set stops at apparent technical levels that market makers can quickly identify and attack. Round numbers, prior highs and lows, and trend lines attract stop clusters, which serve as liquidity sources for institutional investors. Volume-based stop placement avoids the apparent zones.

Even when the analysis is correct, an insufficient buffer space results in premature stop-triggering. Volume-based levels require breathing space since price frequently tries these areas before honoring them. Determine the buffer space based on the average actual range and current volatility trends.

Wrong timing analysis results in bad stop placement judgments. Using 15-minute volume levels for 4-hour trades leads to mismatched expectations and insufficient stop distances. Adjust your stop placement timeframe to reflect your chosen holding period and trading style.

Emotional stop adjustment undermines planned risk management and converts winning methods into losing ones. Once you've discovered a plausible volume-based stop placement, adhere to your strategy regardless of short-term price activity. Emotional adjustments typically result in bigger losses and missed opportunities when the price eventually shifts in your favor.

CHAPTER EIGHT

Entry and Exit Strategies

Precise entry and exit execution distinguishes profitable volume traders from those who comprehend the fundamentals but struggle with implementation. You can find ideal situations, but poor execution will diminish your advantage, converting winning tactics into break-even or losing approaches.

Volume-based entry and exit techniques require a different approach than typical technical analysis methodologies. You're working with zones and probability rather than specific price points, which necessitates flexibility in execution while adhering to rigorous risk management rules.

Precise Entry Techniques with Volume Levels

Volume-based entries aim to be positioned when price interacts with major volume levels rather than predicting exact turning points. The goal is entering with positive risk-to-reward qualities while avoiding hasty positioning, which results in avoidable drawdowns.

POC level entry necessitate patience and perfect timing. When the price approaches the Point of Control, wait for volume confirmation before entering. Increased volume throughout the approach indicates institutional participation, which might result in major price movements. Low volume techniques can produce weak reactions and poor trading outcomes.

Value Area edge entries serve as natural risk-management boundaries for position size. Enter near Value Area High or Low levels, with stops located outside the opposing boundary. This method provides clearly defined risk parameters while positioning for moves back toward the Point of Control.

Scaling into positions is effective with volume profile analysis since volume levels represent zones rather than specific prices. Begin with partial positions when price interacts with significant volume levels, then build on winning positions when volume validates your directional bias.

Stop-Loss Placement That Makes Sense

Volume-based stop placement prioritizes levels where your analysis becomes invalid over arbitrary percentage or pip distances. If you're trading a POC bounce, set your stops where a break of the POC would indicate fundamental shift. This method links your risk management with market realities.

Buffer estimations for volume levels take into account typical market noise and institutional testing. POC levels require additional buffer space than Value Area edges due to increased testing activity. Calculate buffers based on recent volatility metrics rather than fixed pip values.

Multiple Period stop considerations prevent hasty exit from positions with long-term viability. A one-hour POC break may not invalidate a daily Value Area setup. Align your stop placement timing with your targeted holding term and principal analysis timeframe.

Trailing stops and volume levels enable dynamic risk management that responds to changing market conditions. As the price moves in your favor and new volume levels are established, set your stops to these new reference points while maintaining sufficient buffer distance.

Target Selection via Volume Distribution

Volume distribution analysis establishes rational profit targets that are consistent with market structure. The next large volume cluster in your direction serves as the first target, but volume voids indicate areas where price may move fast without resistance.

POC magnetism generates ideal target areas for mean reversion trading. When trading from the Value Area edges, the Point of Control is frequently the primary target because price tends to move toward areas with the biggest volume concentration. This magnetic effect gives consistent earning opportunities.

Volume gap targeting is effective for breakout trades when the price moves beyond established value areas. These gaps represent areas with little prior trading activity, allowing for quick price change until the next major volume cluster.

Multi-target methods maximize profit extraction from volume-based setups. Take partial profits at the first volume-based target, then trail stops for the remaining position toward longer-term volume goals. This strategy maximizes quick income while allowing for longer moves.

Managing Trades As Volume Patterns Change

Volume pattern evolution gives continuous feedback on trade validity and profit possibilities. Increased volume in your favor indicates institutional engagement, which can cause long-term moves. Decreasing volume frequently indicates weakened momentum and potential reversal scenarios.

Real-time volume monitoring allows for more flexible position management as trades develop. When volume climbs dramatically at your target levels, it may signal fresh institutional interest, which could push prices above your initial estimates. Conversely, a drop in volume at targets indicates natural stopping points.

Value Area movements during active trades inform position management choices. If new Value Areas form to your advantage, they provide new reference points for trailing stops and target changes. Value Area moves against your position advise lowering exposure or tightening stops.

Institutional signature identification identifies when major parties are actively involved in your trade direction. Sustained volume at key levels, absorption patterns, and distribution fingerprints all give insight into institutional activity, which influences position management decisions.

The Scalping Approach Versus Swing Approach

Scalping with volume profile focuses on making fast moves between volume levels that are tightly spaced. POC bounces, Value Area edge rejections, and small volume node interactions offer frequent possibilities with limited risk. Success necessitates precise execution with minimum slippage costs.

Scalping periods commonly employ 5-minute to 15-minute charts, with volume analysis from 1-hour and 4-hour timeframes providing context. The goal is to capture fast moves of 10-30 pips while risking 5-15 pips, creating favorable risk-reward ratios and high win rates.

Swing trading with volume profile seeks moves between major volume clusters separated by considerable price differences. These trades could last for days or weeks, necessitating patience and wider stop-loss zones. The strategy is effective for traders who are unable to constantly watch markets.

Swing approach periods are based on daily and weekly volume analysis, using 4-hour charts for exact entry timing. Target moves of 100-300 pips become attainable when trading between big Value Areas or significant POC levels on longer timeframes.

My Biggest Winner with Volume Profile Exits

The trade on EUR/GBP began when the price broke above a weekly Value Area High with significant volume confirmation. My initial target was the next daily POC level, which was roughly 80 pips away, but volume analysis revealed more possibility as the trade progressed.

Instead of taking full profits at my first target, I used volume-based trail stops, which enabled the position to capture a 240-pip move over six days. The key was to identify prolonged institutional volume, which suggested continued purchasing interest above regular profit-taking levels.

Volume absorption patterns at intermediate levels revealed that large players accumulated rather than distributed positions. Each retreat found support in newly created volume clusters, demonstrating the strength of the underlying move and justifying further position holding.

The exit signal occurred when volume patterns moved to distribution characteristics approaching major weekly resistance. Heavy volume at high prices, paired with subsequent weakness, showed institutional selling, prompting a full position exit before the reversal became apparent on price charts alone.

This experience taught me that volume-based exit strategies can capture much greater moves than standard technical analysis methods. The key is to assess institutional behavior via volume patterns rather than relying simply on price-based signals for exit timing.

CHAPTER NINE

Advanced Volume Profiling Techniques

Advanced volume profile techniques differentiate seasoned practitioners from those who simply understand fundamental concepts. These strategies necessitate a deeper understanding of the market and extensive analysis abilities, but they provide significant benefits that warrant the added complexity.

Mastering these advanced tactics requires time and practice. You'll need to acquire insight for how different strategies interact and when specific methods provide the most value. The learning curve is difficult, but the trading benefits are significant.

Multi-Timeframe Volume Analysis

Multi-timeframe volume analysis provides a three-dimensional view of market structure, revealing opportunities that might otherwise be invisible on single-timeframe charts. You're merging volume data from several time periods to better understand both immediate and long-term market trends.

For every shorter time frame analysis, weekly volume profiles provide the structural foundation. These profiles show where institutional money concentrated over time, resulting in reference levels that influence price behavior for months. Weekly POC levels frequently act as significant support and resistance for weeks at a time.

Daily volume analysis refines weekly structure by showing how institutional activity evolves within a larger context. Daily Value Areas that coincide with weekly volume clusters form effective confluence zones. When daily POCs congregate near weekly volume nodes, these levels become key benchmarks.

Intraday volume profiles indicate execution chances in both the daily and weekly structures. The 4-hour and 1-hour volume levels provide precise entry points for trades based on higher timeframe analysis. The trick is to keep perspective on which era drives the underlying trend.

Integration strategies incorporate data from many timeframes without causing chart clutter. Mark only the most important levels from each timeframe with various colors or line styles. Too many volume levels lead to confusion rather than clarity in decision-making.

Volume Profiles in Ranging and Trending Markets

Ranging markets have distinctive volume act profile patterns that are very different from trending conditions. During consolidation periods, volume is concentrated in the middle of price ranges, with a generally even distribution above and below the Point of Control. These balanced profiles point to efficient price discovery.

Value Area overlap in range marketplaces show markets where fair market consensus values exist. Multiple trading sessions with overlapping Value Areas demonstrate that buyers and sellers may agree on reasonable pricing within set parameters. These overlaps frequently indicate continuing consolidation.

With concentration gradually changing in the trend direction, trending markets show skewed volume distributions. Healthy uptrends show volume clustering at higher price levels within each profile period. When this pattern breaks down, trend continuance becomes uncertain.

Volume-based trend strength measurement focuses on how volume is distributed during trending periods. Strong trends show an increase in volume at successively higher or lower price levels. Weak trends show volume concentration that does not move with price direction.

Combining Volume Profile and Price Action Signals

Price action confirmation improves volume profile analysis by delivering entry timing cues at volume-based levels. Candlestick patterns, support and resistance tests, and momentum divergences combine with volume analysis to provide comprehensive trading techniques.

Rejection signals at volume levels provide high-probability entry points. When price approaches a major POC or Value Area edge and exhibits clear rejection in the form of pin bars, shooting stars, or hammer formations, powerful trade setups with predetermined risk criteria emerge.

Breakout confirmation utilizing the volume profile eliminates spurious breakout losses. Traditional breakouts frequently fail, but when supplemented with volume analysis to show sustained institutional participation, breakout success rates rise dramatically. Watch for volume increases during breakaway attempts.

Momentum divergence at volume levels indicates possible reversal opportunities. When price establishes new highs or lows but volume fails to confirm the move at substantial volume levels, divergence patterns frequently result in mean reversion trades back to established value areas.

News Event Trading: Volume Preparation

Pre-event volume analysis illustrates how institutional money was positioned prior to big economic pronouncements. These positioning patterns frequently forecast post-announcement price movement more accurately than the actual news outcome. Smart money often has a better understanding of outcome probability than retail traders.

Value Area positioning ahead of news events gives critical context for analyzing market reactions. When prices trade at Value Area extremes before to important announcements, it indicates institutional bias in certain directions. Post-announcement movements frequently accelerate in the direction of pre-positioning.

The discovery of volume voids illustrates where rapid price changes are most likely to occur following news releases. Areas with low volume concentration provide routes of least resistance for turbulent post-announcement price behavior. These vacancies frequently serve as targets for first news-driven swings.

Post-event volume analysis helps identify whether news-driven shifts have institutional support to continue. Sustained volume during post-announcement price action implies that actual money is driving the move. Low volume movements frequently revert fast when emotional emotions diminish.

The Composite Volume Approach to Improve Accuracy

Composite volume profiles use various time periods to illustrate long-term institutional positioning patterns. Instead of assessing individual trading sessions, composite profiles combine volume data from multiple days or weeks to show cumulative institutional activity.

Weekly composite profiles smooth out daily volatility noise, revealing underlying institutional positioning tendencies. These profiles frequently show accumulation or distribution patterns that are not obvious in daily analysis. Monthly composites provide an even larger view of institutional activity cycles.

Rolling composite profiles are updated on a constant basis, incorporating fresh data while removing previous eras.

This dynamic approach will show how institutional posture changes over time while remaining sensitive to recent developments. 10-day rolling composites are ideal for intermediate-term analysis.

Seasonal composite analysis identifies repeating volume patterns that are related to calendar influences, central bank meeting cycles, or economic announcement dates. These patterns can assist traders estimate when volume characteristics are expected to change and alter their trading tactics accordingly.

Advanced Patterns that Most Traders Never See

Double distribution profiles show two distinct volume clusters separated by low-volume areas. These patterns frequently emerge during transitional market periods, when old and new value areas vie for dominance. The resolution typically leads to a considerable directional move.

Volume migration patterns indicate shifting institutional sentiment before visible trend shifts. Institutional money is repositioning when volume concentrations gradually move from one area to another over several sessions. These movements frequently precede large structural shifts.

Absorption patterns form when one side of the market absorbs all available volume from the other without causing significant price movement. These patterns generate imbalances, which are finally resolved by quick price adjustments to new equilibrium levels.

Failed auction patterns emerge when prices attempt to create value in new areas but are repeatedly rejected and returned to old zones. Multiple failed auctions at the same levels frequently indicate strong institutional protection, which leads to eventual reversals.

Institutional footprint analysis combines volume profile and order flow data to identify significant player activity characteristics. While most retail traders do not have access to comprehensive order flow, volume profile patterns frequently show signs of institutional accumulation and distribution activities.

CHAPTER TEN

Putting It All Together—Your Trading Plan

Developing a systematic trading plan involves combining all volume profile elements into a cohesive approach that is tailored to your personality, available time, and risk tolerance. Clear guidelines for analysis, entry, management, and exit decisions are required to remove emotional influence from the trading process.

Understanding volume profile principles and implementing them profitably necessitate the establishment of an organized approach. Many traders fail because they switch between approaches without giving any one approach enough time to demonstrate its effectiveness.

Create Your Personal Volume Profile Trading System

Your unique trading system must be compatible with your lifestyle and psychological makeup. Focus on high time frame analysis using profile volume charts if you can only check charts twice a week. Active traders who regularly monitor markets can use shorter timeframe approaches to capture more frequent chances.

Market selection has a considerable impact on system design. Major currency pairs, such as EUR/USD and GBP/USD, provide the most consistent volume data and clearest volume profile patterns. Exotic pairs frequently show irregular volume characteristics, making reliable analysis difficult.

Risk tolerance dictates the proper position size and stop-loss distances. Conservative traders should focus on high-probability setups with tight stops near volume levels. When trading major volume confluences, aggressive traders can use larger stops and position sizes.

Time horizon preferences influence the timeframe used for your primary analysis. Day traders focus on 1-hour and 4-hour volume profiles with high time frame context. Swing traders focus on daily and weekly volume analysis in conjunction with intraday charts to ensure exact timing.

Daily Routine & Market Preparation

Effective volume profile trading necessitates continuous market preparation processes that identify opportunities and set reference levels before trading begins. Your preparation should include numerous timeframes and a focus on the most important volume-based levels for the forthcoming session.

Weekly preparation entails analyzing major currency pairings for structural changes in volume distribution. Mark notable weekly POC levels, Value Area boundaries, and volume clusters that may influence next week's price behavior. These levels provide the foundation for all shorter time frame analysis.

Daily preparation improves the weekly analysis by identifying new volume levels and updating current reference points. Check for any overnight changes that may have resulted in new volume signatures or invalidated earlier levels. Update your charts to reflect updated Value Areas and POC positions.

Session preparation is focused on the individual trading session in which you will act. Trading prospects are impacted by the distinctive volume patterns of the Asian, London, and New York session. Determine which volume levels are most likely to be tested during active trading hours.

Trade Management: Entry to Exit

Emotional decision-making is removed from position management through systematic trade management. Once you've entered a trade based on volume profile analysis, you should follow preset guidelines for position sizing, stop changes, and profit-taking.

Entry execution necessitates patience and discipline in order to await favorable conditions. Do not force trades when volume confirmation is poor or when price reaches volume levels with low probability features. Missing mediocre setups saves capital for high-probability opportunities.

Position sizing should include setup quality and market volatility. Use larger positions for trades with multiple volume confirmations and tighter stop limits. Reduce position size when trading in volatile markets or when volume confirmation is marginal.

Stop-loss management uses volume-based logic rather than emotional reactions. Stops should only be adjusted when volume analysis changes, not in response to short-term price volatility. Premature stop changes typically result in higher losses and lost profits.

Profit-taking strategies. Use volume distribution to determine your exit timing. Take partial profits at the first volume-based objectives while following stops on remaining positions. Complete exits occur when volume patterns indicate institutional distribution or structural changes.

Common Mistakes and How I Overcome Them

Overanalyzing charts with too many volume indicators leads to confusion rather than clarity. I learned to focus on the most important levels from each timeframe while ignoring tiny volume clusters that have no bearing on major price moves. Simplicity generally yields better results than complication.

When volume confirmation is weak, forcing trades leads to unneeded losses. During my early volume profile trading, I took positions based on partial indications rather than waiting for entire setups. Patience increased my win rate dramatically while decreasing emotional stress.

Ignoring greater timeframe context leads to poor trade selection and timing. Even the best 1-hour volume setups can fail if they contradict with the daily or weekly volume structure. Before committing funds to any trade, always investigate greater timeframes.

Inadequate position sizing in relation to setup quality results in lost profit chances or increased risk. High-probability volume confluences warrant larger positions, whereas marginal setups necessitate smaller sizes. Match your position size to your level of strength and confidence.

Increasing Confidence in Your Volume Analysis

Confidence in volume profile analysis grows with constant application and result tracking. Keep detailed records of your volume-based trading decisions and outcomes. This literature helps you identify which trading tactics are most effective for your trading style and market conditions.

Paper trading with volume profile analysis provides experience without risking funds. Practice identifying setups, placing theoretical trades, and managing positions using your planned system. This practice phase identifies flaws in your approach before they cost you money.

Gradual implementation protects you from becoming overwhelmed with too many new concepts at once. Begin with basic POC and Value Area analysis before on to more complex methodologies. Before attempting sophisticated multi-timeframe or composite analysis approaches, ensure that you properly understand the underlying ideas.

Result measurement focuses on risk-adjusted returns rather than win rates. A system with 60% wins that captures huge moves while reducing losses will frequently outperform an 80% win rate system with inadequate risk-to-reward ratios. Track your typical risk-to-reward ratios based on setup type.

Your Next Steps for Consistent Profitability

Consistent profitability through volume profile analysis necessitates time, practice, and reasonable expectations. Most traders require six months to a year of focused practice to become successful with volume-based trading strategies. Don't expect immediate perfection or constant income during the learning process.

Begin with one currency pair and one timeframe until you understand the fundamental ideas. EUR/USD on 4-hour charts gives good learning possibilities due to consistent volume data and distinct patterns. As your skills improve, gradually increase the level of intricacy.

Concentrate on process improvement rather than short-term results. Perfect execution of your volume profile system will eventually result in profits, but focusing too heavily on quick results causes emotional distraction, which lowers decision-making quality.

Continuous learning and adaption. Maintain your volume profile abilities as markets evolve. Volume patterns vary depending on market conditions, central bank policy, and technology advancements. Maintain your flexibility and willingness to alter your approach as your experience grows and market conditions change.

The route to volume profile mastery is difficult yet rewarding. You now have the tools and expertise to view markets through institutional lenses and position yourself where actual money flows. Your success is contingent on consistent application, focused execution, and steady skill growth over time.

Video Access page

Thank you for purchasing my book! As a gesture of appreciation, I'm excited to share exclusive video content created just for you.

To access your free videos, simply visit:

https://drive.google.com/drive/folders/1Ok72XbvqGGbtXIaGME3DiCtcdQUoxN0w?usp=drive_link

I sincerely appreciate your support and hope these extra resources make your reading experience even more valuable!

Best regards,

Nathaniel J. Brooks

www.ingramcontent.com/pod-product-compliance
Lightning Source LLC
LaVergne TN
LVHW022108200926
848481LV00003B/1105